Living Bread Crumbs
A Healing Journey

Della Norwood Smith

DEDICATION

I dedicate this book to Jesus Christ, the Bread of Life.

And Jesus said unto them, I am the bread of life: he that cometh to me shall never hunger; and he that believeth on me shall never thirst. John 6:33-35

CONTENTS

Acknowledgments   i

1   Oh God   1

2   A Tear Fell   2

3   Empty   3

4   Scars   4

5   Need A Friend?   6

6   Bitter Seed   8

7   Used   10

8   Brave   12

9   The Cracked Pot   13

10   Childless   14

11   Regarding Fathers   16

ACKNOWLEDGMENTS

First, I would like to acknowledge my Heavenly Father for inspiring these words through His Word. And Jesus Christ for taking my broken heart and making it whole. And Holy Spirit for being my comforter and teacher.

I would like to acknowledge my great aunt Irma Yarborough who encouraged me to publish my poetry many years ago. She did not live to see it, but I know she's watching from heaven and smiling.

I would also like to thank my church family at Lion Gate Church who saw this book even before I did and encouraged me to make it a reality.

1.
OH GOD

Oh God, how many times have you heard this prayer?
Pleading for comfort in the midst of despair?
Whenever all traces of hope seem to be gone
Please God, give me the strength to trudge on

Give me some patience from your reserve
And a little wisdom, and maybe some courage
Give me a shoulder to catch my tears
Give me the peace to quell my fears

Sometimes I feel so helpless and small
Like my life doesn't make any difference at all
Please God, whenever I'm feeling this way
Just help me make it through the day

———◆┃◆———

God is our refuge and strength, a very present help in trouble.
Psalms 46:1

2.
A TEAR FELL

A tear fell
A heart broke
But as it fell
A prayer it wrote

For the strongest prayers
Are without words
A prayer of tears
Is always heard

———◆◆———

Thou tellest my wanderings:
put thou my tears in thy bottle:
are they not in thy book?
Psalms 56:8

3.
EMPTY

Empty longing
In my soul
Needing something
To be whole

Fleeting feeling
Comes and goes
Always comes back
I suppose

Simple surrender
I give up
I receive
God's great love

Now I know
What it was
I was missing
Holy Love

——◆▮◆——

That Christ may dwell in your hearts by faith; that ye, being rooted and grounded in love, may be able to comprehend with all the saints what is the breadth, and length, and depth, and height; and to know the love of Christ, which passeth knowledge, that ye might be filled with all the fulness of God. Ephesians 3:17-19

4.
SCARS

Everyone has scars
Some are deep within
Some are easier to see
Like the one that's on my chin

I got it from a bicycle
When I was still quite small
And though you still can see it
It doesn't hurt at all

And then there was that time
That someone broke my heart
I didn't see it coming
And it ripped my world apart

Some of us were wounded
From betrayal by a friend
A deep cut made by broken trust
Is difficult to mend

Rejection and abandonment
Have wounded many more
We all long for acceptance
It's deep within our core

I'm sure your scars are different
Perhaps some are the same
But there's healing for them all
It's found in Jesus' name

He was wounded for our transgressions
He was bruised to bear our shame
The stripes upon his bleeding back
Were endured for every pain

Even the daggered thorns he wore
Paid the price for peace of mind
The blood he shed was offered
For the healing of all mankind

It's simple to receive it
Although sometimes it's hard
To trust and let our walls down
Because of all the scars

But he will never harm you
He knows the scars you bear
If you need proof of his pure love
Look at the scars he wears

———◆I◆———

See, I have engraved you on the palms of my hands; your walls are ever before me.
Isaiah 49:16

He is despised and rejected of men; a man of sorrows, and acquainted with grief: and we
hid as it were our faces from him; he was despised, and we esteemed him not. Surely he
hath born our griefs, and carried our sorrows: yet we did esteem him stricken, smitten of
God, and afflicted. But he was wounded for our transgressions, he was bruised for our
iniquities: the chastisement of our peace was upon him; and with his stripes we are healed.
Isaiah 53:3-5

5.
NEED A FRIEND?

You find yourself feeling empty inside
And you try to cover your pain with your pride
Like the sad clown who paints a smile on his face
And cheers those around him, but can never erase
The emptiness that haunts and taunts him always

You've learned from life that you've got to be tough
You've got to be strong when the going gets rough
You've hardened your heart in self-defense
And you're afraid you'll be hurt if you take another chance
But deep inside there's a tender child who still longs to dance

You wander through life going nowhere
Sometimes you get weary and just sit and stare
Is there an answer to why you're here?
Are you just meant to suffer and then disappear?
Is there anyone out there who possibly cares?

You've been hurt by so many wrongs
You just can't let go, the pain's been there too long
Loneliness is your closest friend
And disappointment lurks around every bend
If this is life, who cares if it ends?

Well, THERE IS someone who cares that you hurt
He knows how it feels to be treated like dirt
He's been put down and hated, criticized and abused
He suffered rejection and betrayal too

He was stripped of his dignity and stripped of his clothes
Abandoned by his friends, and seized by his foes
He's been lonely and weary and hungry and cold
He never married, he had no one to hold

"Who in the world would care?" you may say
Well, his name is Jesus, and he's alive today!
He's waiting to hear you call out his name
He'll fill you with love and heal your shame

He walked this earth in the body of a man
So he could really understand
Our hopes, our joys, our fears, our pain
He felt it all, his loss was our gain

Call out for grace and mercy too
And receive the joy that's waiting for you!

———◆◖◗◆———

For we have not an high priest which cannot be touched with the feeling of our infirmities;
but was in all points tempted like as we are, yet without sin. Let us come boldly unto the
throne of grace, that we may obtain mercy, and find grace to help in time of need.
Hebrews 4:15-16

6.
BITTER SEED

Words were said
The pain went deep
I tossed and turned
I couldn't sleep

The more I thought
The more I burned
My anger grew
My stomach churned

The thoughts kept coming
To my mind
Why did you treat me
So unkind?

A bitter seed
Went in my heart
Would I let it grow?
Or stop its start?

As I pondered
What to do
I heard your words
The words of truth

"A bitter root
Will many defile
For its poison spreads
To many lives"

I made a choice
To pull that weed
To stop its start
While still a seed

I prayed for the one
Who hurt me so
And as I did
Forgiveness flowed

Not all at once
It took some time
But as I obeyed
Your grace was mine

Now I am free
The turmoil's passed
Your peace has come
I'm free at last

———◆❙◆———

Follow peace with all men, and holiness, without which no man shall see the Lord: Looking diligently lest any man fail of the grace of God; lest any root of bitterness springing up trouble you, and thereby many be defiled. Hebrews 12:14-15

7.
USED

Used
Abused
Rejected
Forsaken

Love
Not love
Not real
Mistaken

Ashamed
Full of pain
Heart sad
Broken

Tried again
Didn't win
Hard heart
Won't be broken

Heart healed
God is real
Hope restored
By my Savior

Healed heart
New start
Freedom found
In my Savior

Chains gone
New song
Praises to
God my Savior

Now I'm used
Not abused
Love to serve
God my Savior

———◆◆◆———

He health the broken in heart, and bindeth up their wounds.
Psalms 147:3

8.
BRAVE

Brave one, strong one
Not so brave. Weak.
It's okay to crumble
When you're at my feet

My grace is all sufficient
It's perfect when you're not
It's enough that I work through you
I would rather a cracked pot

For flaws allow My beauty
To shine through broken places
And all along the path you run
You water other racers

I AM with you always
And yes, I know you know
But I wanted to remind you
I'm going where you go

———◆◆◆———

And he said unto me, My grace is sufficient for thee: for my strength is made perfect in weakness. Most gladly therefore will I rather glory in my infirmities, that the power of Christ may rest upon me. 2 Corinthians 12:9

———◆◆◆———

The following story is what sparked the inspiration for the poem "Brave." I don't know the origin of the story, so I'm not sure who to give the credit to, but it's a beautiful life lesson for us all.

9.
THE CRACKED POT

A water bearer in India had two large pots, each hung on each end of a pole which he carried across his neck. One of the pots had a crack in it, and while the other pot was perfect and always delivered a full portion of water at the end of the long walk from the stream to the master's house, the cracked pot arrived only half full.

For a full two years this went on daily, with the bearer delivering only one and a half pots full of water in his master's house. Of course, the perfect pot was proud of its accomplishments. But the poor cracked pot was ashamed of its own imperfections, and miserable that it was able to accomplish only half of what it had been made to do.

After two years of what it perceived to be a bitter failure, it spoke to the water bearer one day by the stream. "I am ashamed of myself, and I want to apologize to you." "Why?" asked the bearer. "What are you ashamed of?" I have been able, for these past two years, to deliver only half my load because this crack in my side causes water to leak out all the way back to your master's house. Because of my flaws, you have to do all of this work and you don't get full value for your efforts," the pot said.

The water bearer felt sorry for the old cracked pot and in his compassion, he said, "As we return to the master's house, I want you to notice the beautiful flowers along the path." Indeed, as they went up the hill, the old cracked pot took notice of the sun warming the beautiful wild flowers on the side of the path, and this cheered it some. But at the end of the trail, it still felt bad because it had leaked out half its load, and so again it apologized to the bearer for its failure.

The bearer said to the pot, "Did you notice that there were flowers only on your side of the path but not on the other pot's side? That's because I have always known about your flaw, and I took advantage of it. I planted flower seeds on your side of the path, and every day while we walk back from the stream, you've watered them. For two years I have been able to pick these beautiful flowers to decorate my master's table. Without you being just the way you are, he would not have this beauty to grace his house."

Each of us has our own unique flaws. We're all cracked pots. But if we will allow it, the Lord will use our flaws to grace His Father's table. In God's great economy, nothing goes to waste. So, as we seek ways to minister together and as God calls you to the tasks He has appointed for you, don't be afraid of your flaws. Acknowledge them and allow Him to take advantage of them, and you, too, can be the cause of beauty in His pathway.

10.
CHILDLESS

For all the barren wombs
That never bore a child

For all the ones whose choices
Caused their child to die

For all the ones who gave birth
But gave their child away

For all the grieving mothers
Whose child lays in the grave

The Lord has not forgotten
The pain and grief you bear

The longing for your children
When your children are not there

You are not a second class
Forsaken and alone

He feels the beating of your hurt
He hears your silent moan

There is healing for your soul
Whatever pain you have

If you'll bring it to Jesus
He'll apply his healing salve

━━◆◙◆━━

There are three things that are never satisfied, yea, four things that say not, It is enough: the grave; and the barren womb; the earth that is not filled with water; and the fire that saith not, It is enough. Proverbs 30:15-16

In Rama was there a voice heard, lamentation, and weeping, and great mourning, Rachel weeping for her children, and would not be comforted, because they are not. Matthew 2:18

11.
REGARDING FATHERS

If you had a father
You loved with all your heart
The honor will come easy
You got a real good start

But many hearts were broken
By a father here below
Perhaps they were just missing
Perhaps they dealt cruel blows

On Father's Day we think of them
With gratitude or pain
But here we are because they are
This truth will still remain

It's right to honor fathers
There's a promise that comes with it
A life that's long and goes well
It's in the sixth commandment

If it's hard for you to honor
The father you were given
There is healing for your wounded soul
From Father God in heaven

He wants to mend those places
That were marred by earthly flaws
His love for you is greater
Than you ever knew there was

Don't be afraid to trust Him
He's not like earthly men
His love is unconditional
No matter where you've been

If you've been running from Him
Because of pain or loss
Consider running to Him
There's healing at the cross

———◆◆◆———

When my father and my mother forsake me, then the LORD will take me up.
Psalm 27:10

ABOUT THE AUTHOR

I WILL SING THE LORD'S PRAISE,
FOR HE HAS BEEN GOOD TO ME.

PSALM 13:6

Della Smith has been writing poetry since she was a
teenager, including the first poem in this book. However,
after a radical heart healing encounter with Jesus Christ,
her poetry dramatically changed in content and flows from
her relationship with our Heavenly Father, His Son Jesus
Christ and the Holy Spirit.

Della lives in Baton Rouge, Louisiana
with her husband of more than 30 years.

For more of Della's poetry, visit her website at:
www.livingbreadcrumbs.com

www.ingramcontent.com/pod-product-compliance
Lightning Source LLC
Chambersburg PA
CBHW031618040426
42452CB00006B/588